FOOD
AND
DRINK
IN
BRITAIN

Jackie Maguire

Oxford Bookworms
Factfiles

OXFORD
UNIVERSITY PRESS

Great Clarendon Street, Oxford OX2 6DP

Oxford University Press is a department of the University of Oxford.
It furthers the University's objective of excellence in research, scholarship,
and education by publishing worldwide in

Oxford New York

Auckland Cape Town Dar es Salaam Hong Kong Karachi
Kuala Lumpur Madrid Melbourne Mexico City Nairobi
New Delhi Shanghai Taipei Toronto

With offices in

Argentina Austria Brazil Chile Czech Republic France Greece
Guatemala Hungary Italy Japan Poland Portugal Singapore
South Korea Switzerland Thailand Turkey Ukraine Vietnam

OXFORD and OXFORD ENGLISH are registered trade marks of
Oxford University Press in the UK and in certain other countries

© Oxford University Press 2000

The moral rights of the author have been asserted
Database right Oxford University Press (maker)

First published 2000
2009 2008 2007
10 9 8 7 6

ISBN-13: 978 0 19 422869 5

Printed in China

ACKNOWLEDGEMENTS

The publishers would like to thank the following for the permission to reproduce
photographs: Anthony Blake Photolibrary pp 8 (sausage, mash and
beans/Neville Kuypers), 9 (roast beef meal/Sian Irvine, packed lunch/
Joy Skipper), 10 (roast lamb meal), 12 (picnic/Gerrit Buntrock),
16 (pot food/Joy Skipper, baked potato/Tony Robins, sandwiches/PFT
Associates), 19 (mashed potato/Sian Irvine), 21 (trifle), 22 (beer
garden/Mark Turner), 24 (tea), 26 (shepherds pie); Cephas Picture
Library pp 7 (strawberry picking/Diana Mewes), 13 (barbecue/Mick
Rock, people picnicking/Nigel Blythe), 16 (fish and chips/Nigel
Blythe), 21 (ice cream van/Hazel Smith), 23 (dart game/John
Heinrich); Corel p 7 (cows); Food Features p5 (supermarket),
6 (fish counter), 10 (roast pork, pudding), 11 (school cafeteria),
19 (roast potatoes), 20 (cakes), 23 (bar in pub), 27 (scone); Goodshoot
pp 3 (oysters), 8 (toast and cereal); Impact Photos pp 11 (China
Town/Mark Henley), 24 (tea break/Mark Cator); RSPCA Photolibrary
p 5 (battery hens/Tom Claxton); Sally & Richard Greenhill p 24
(woman having tea); Stockbyte pp 1 (roast beef), 3 (nuts), 8 (cooked
breakfast), 9 (peas, onion, cabbage), 17 (fish and chips); Telegraph
Colour Library p 3 (woman standing next to fridge/FPG
International); Tessa Traeger Photo Library pp 2 (curing fish),
4 (market), 6 (fishermen), 19 (potatoes)

Illustrations by: Mike Ogden.

OXFORD BOOKWORMS

For a full list of titles in all the Oxford Bookworms series, please refer to the Oxford ELT catalogue (or online at www.oup.com/elt).

1 Introduction

Although Britain is quite a small country, it offers a wide choice of food and drink. The types of food people eat have changed a lot over the years for several reasons. People have come to Britain from different parts of the world, bringing their favourite food with them and often opening restaurants. British people have travelled to other countries and brought new foods back home. And today big supermarket companies can buy food from all over the world and sell it while it is still good to eat.

In Britain you can find traditional food like roast beef or fish and chips – and vegetarian food for those who do not eat meat. As well as foods from different parts of Britain, you can buy Italian, Mexican and West Indian food. Tea is often described as the national drink, but in Britain's pubs you can drink beers and wines from many different countries as well as cider from the West Country and whisky from Scotland.

In this book we will look at some of the different things the British eat and drink today. There are recipes too, to show you how to make some traditional British food yourself.

Roast beef

2 Changes in diet and shopping

Britain is an island between the North Sea and the Atlantic Ocean, and for those who live near the sea, fish and shellfish have always been important. Before people had fridges to keep food cold and fresh, they started to keep fish from going bad by salting, drying or smoking it.

One thing which has changed is the way some foods are seen as ordinary and cheap, and others special and valuable. Shellfish like oysters used to be popular with poor people because anyone could go to a beach and pick them up, for free. Today they are harder to find and usually quite expensive.

Away from the sea, people first ate wild animals, but then hundreds of years ago they began keeping sheep, cows and chickens on farms. Farmers have grown fruit, vegetables and cereals (for making bread) for centuries too. During the Middle Ages (eleventh to fifteenth centuries), ships brought sugar, nuts and spices from far away. The spices were often used to

A fridge-freezer in 1950

Smoked fish

hide the taste of food which was going bad! When sailors went to foreign places, they brought back more kinds of food. At first only rich people could buy the things brought from overseas, but slowly they became cheaper and easier to find.

When gas and electricity came into people's houses, cooking became much easier, and fridges and freezers meant people could keep food much longer.

The diet of many British people is quite different to that of their parents and has often changed in their own lifetime. Those who lived during the Second World War (1939–1945) can remember when there was not a lot of food to choose from. Fruit like bananas and oranges

Nuts

An oyster

A greengrocer's market stall

were very difficult to find, and each person could have only fifty grams of butter and sugar each week.

Today we have many more fruits and other foods to choose from and new ways to cook them, like microwave ovens. But we have less time for shopping and cooking.

People used to walk to their nearest shops almost every day. They went to the baker's for bread, the butcher's for meat, the greengrocer's for fruit and vegetables and so on. Now they drive to supermarkets where they can buy everything under one roof. The very big supermarkets, or superstores, sell over 20,000 different products, including food from Africa, Asia and the Americas. Many of the small shops have lost so much business that they have closed down.

We also know more about health and the body today. Children grow up learning that some foods are good for us while others, for example some sugars and fats, are bad. Some people have tried to change their diet to eat healthier food and most shopping centres have health food shops which sell lots of different natural foods.

Some people, called vegetarians, choose not to eat meat for a number of different reasons. Some do not like it, some think it is wrong to kill and eat animals, some think it is too expensive or just not safe. There are several different kinds of vegetarians: those who eat fish but no meat, those who eat eggs and dairy products (things which come from milk, like butter and cheese) but no meat, and those who do not eat any animal or anything which comes from an animal – so no meat, no fish, no milk and no eggs. They eat fruit, vegetables, nuts, bread, rice, etc.

People have been vegetarians all round the world for thousands of years, and in Britain the number has grown quite a lot recently. This is partly because some people have become ill and even died after eating

Fruit and vegetables in a supermarket

A battery chicken

unsafe food. Another reason is that many people do not like the way animals are farmed. Examples of this are battery chickens, or young cows kept in the dark so their meat stays light in colour. About 5% of people in Britain today do not eat any meat, about 10% do not eat red meat, and most people say they eat less meat now than in the past. If a food is suitable for vegetarians, the packet often has the letter 'V' on it, and vegetarian meals on a menu often have the 'V' next to them to help people choose what to eat.

3 Farming and fishing

Before British farmers decide what to plant or what animals to keep, they must think about the weather, the kind of land and whether it is flat or hilly, and how much money they can make. Some farmers have only crops (plants grown for food) or animals (like cows and sheep) but many have mixed farms – they grow some crops and keep some animals too.

Although Britain is mild (it never gets very hot or very cold) the weather does differ from one part of the country to another; the east for example, is drier and the west is wetter. In the hills of Scotland and Wales it rains a lot, so the grass grows well and there are more sheep. In the south it is sunnier and drier so more fruit, vegetables and cereals are grown. Different fruit and vegetables grow well in different areas –

A fish counter　　　*Landing fish*

potatoes grow well on the flat land of the east of England; apples and soft fruits, like strawberries, grow well in Kent (in south-east England) and in parts of the Midlands (in central England). Because of this, there are many farms where you can pick your own fruit and vegetables. This is often much cheaper than buying from a supermarket, and people like to know they are eating food at its freshest.

Fishing is also very important in Britain, but over-fishing and pollution have made life difficult.

British fishermen have had many disagreements with fishermen from other countries about who can catch fish. There are not enough fish in the sea for everyone, so governments must try to agree on how much fish each country can catch. Fishermen have to think about the present and the future: they need to make money today, but they also need to feed their families tomorrow.

Although there are many types of fish in British waters, in many sea-side towns the tourist business now brings in more money than fishing.

Picking strawberries　　　*Cows on a country road*

4 Home-cooked food

Some people like to 'go to work on an egg' – they eat an egg for breakfast before going to work. But many more breakfast on cereal – often cornflakes – while others have toast with butter and marmalade. And, whatever they eat, most people drink tea or coffee.

At weekends many people have a more traditional, cooked breakfast. If you stay in a hotel or a 'B & B' (Bed and Breakfast), you can have a breakfast like this.

Some people have their biggest meal in the middle of the day and some have it in the evening, but most people today have a small mid-day meal – usually sandwiches, and perhaps some crisps and some fruit.

The evening meal is usually called 'tea' or 'dinner'. A traditional British dinner is meat and two vegetables. The most popular meats are chicken, beef (from a cow), pork (from a pig) and lamb (from a young sheep). Vegetables grown in Britain, like potatoes, carrots, peas, cabbage and onions, are very popular, but today you can buy vegetables from many countries all through the year.

Two favourite meals with children are fish fingers and chips, and baked beans on toast. Baked beans, first sold in Boston, USA, but

Cereal and toast

A cooked breakfast

Bangers, beans and mash

Peas, onions and cabbage

A child's lunch box

now very popular in Britain, are cheap to buy and quick to heat up. There are several different kinds, and they are eaten at almost any time – for breakfast, lunch or dinner!

Three traditional British meals are: bangers, beans and mash (sausages, baked beans and mashed potato), stew (meat

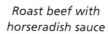

Roast beef with horseradish sauce

cooked with lots of vegetables), and the Sunday roast. Sunday is a day when many families like to enjoy a big meal together. They usually have a big piece of meat which is roasted (cooked in the oven for about two hours) with potatoes. Beef is eaten with hot white horseradish sauce, pork with sweet apple sauce,

Lamb with mint sauce

Roast pork with apple sauce

and lamb with green mint sauce – perhaps made with mint grown in the garden.

After dinner, people eat dessert – something sweet like fruit, chocolate cake, or apple pie.

Many people do not have time to cook traditional food today, so they

Apple and blackberry pie

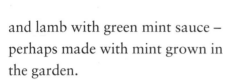

buy food which is ready to eat or quick to make, but visitors to Britain often want to try 'typical' British food. The best place to go is usually a pub and many pubs have a notice outside saying: 'home cooked food'. One of the best known pub meals is the ploughman's lunch. A ploughman was someone who, years ago, worked in the fields, so his midday meal was simple: some bread, cheese, tomatoes and some salad.

And where do people eat their food when they are at home? Breakfast is usually a quick meal, eaten in the kitchen. Lunch is often eaten at school or work. Dinner may be eaten in the kitchen, the dining-room, or the living-room – often in front of the television!

5 Eating out and eating outside

Going to a restaurant for a meal, instead of eating at home, is called 'eating out'. Only a few years ago this was too expensive for most people; today the British do it a lot more often and there are many different kinds of places to go.

Walk through any town centre today and you will find coffee shops where you can buy a drink and perhaps a sandwich or cake; snack-bars where you can get light meals; and waiter-service restaurants where someone takes your order and brings the food to your table.

Schools, colleges, companies, etc. usually have a self-service restaurant called a cafeteria where you buy your food and take it back to your table. An evening meal in a restaurant

Restaurants in Chinatown

usually has three courses. The first course is quite a small one called a starter. It may be something like a soup or salad or some sea-food. The next course is the main course and is the biggest of the three. This is usually meat or fish with vegetables, or vegetarian food. The last course is either something sweet – a dessert, like fruit, cake, or a piece of pie – or a cheese plate, which is pieces of different cheeses with biscuits and grapes. Some people have both! The meal usually finishes with tea or coffee and perhaps a mint chocolate.

All three courses can be hot or cold, and if the main meal comes with

A school cafeteria

potatoes you can choose which kind you would like. With beef and sometimes fish, you are asked how you would like it cooked: well-done (cooked for a long time), medium, or rare (not cooked for long). In the bigger cities you can find restaurants with mostly fish or vegetarian dishes, or food from other countries. Chinese and Indian restaurants have long been popular in Britain, but people love going to other kinds of restaurants, like Thai, Turkish, Moroccan or French. Although you can find these restaurants in most places, there are certain areas of London where you can find many together. In Chinatown, for example, you can find food from many parts of China, and in the West End there are a lot of Thai restaurants. Indian food is by far the most popular, and there

are many Indian restaurants in Wembley, Southall and the East End of London.

Indian food comes from the south Asian countries of Pakistan, Nepal, Bangladesh and Sri Lanka as well as India. In 1950, when most Indian restaurants were run by people from Asia, there were only about 300 Indian restaurants in Britain. In the 1950s and 1960s many people moved

Picnic in the country

Picnicking at a musical evening

classes in Britain for people to learn how to cook Indian food and there is even a National Curry Day!

During the summer, some restaurants and pubs have tables outside, on the street or in a garden. Britain is famous for its rain, so if the weather is good, many people like to enjoy fresh air and sunshine with their meal.

from south Asia to Britain and in the seventies and eighties Indian food became much more popular.

A barbecue

People often take their own food to a park or a beach, and sit on the grass or the sand. Picnics like this may be very simple – just some sandwiches, crisps and hot tea – or a bit more special, with smoked fish, strawberries and champagne. Sometimes people take picnics when they go to watch outdoor sports or go to musical evenings in parks.

Today there are over 8,000 Indian restaurants in Britain and many are run by British Asians – people born in Britain to Asian parents. The most common Indian dish is a curry, which is meat, fish or vegetables cooked with different spices. One of the most popular Indian dishes in Britain is *chicken tikka masala* which is pieces of chicken in a spicy sauce, and not a traditional Indian dish at all, but a British-Indian invention!

There are now many evening

Over the past few years, barbecuing food has become more popular and all sorts of food can be cooked in this way.

FOOD MAP OF
THE BRITISH ISLES

Whisky

Dundee cake

SCOTLAND

Dundee

NORTHERN

Shortbread

6 Fast food

'Today's newspaper is tomorrow's fish and chip wrapper,' people used to say. Why? Because years ago, fish and chips were packed in newspaper to keep them warm until they were eaten. This does not happen any more, for health reasons, but fish and chips is still Britain's most famous fast food.

Fried fish and cooked potatoes were first sold in the streets of London and other cities in the 1850s, and the first fish and chip shops were opened in the 1860s. The most popular kind of fish used is cod, but other white fish are also used. The fish is cooked in hot fat and is usually eaten with chips on which people put salt and brown vinegar, and/or tomato sauce, or even curry sauce. Some people eat bread and butter, with their fish and chips, or soft peas called mushy peas. Fish and chips is very popular with holiday-makers at the sea-side (even if the weather is so cold that they have to eat them sitting in their cars!) or at the weekend as a change

Buying fish and chips

from cooking at home.

A favourite snack (quick food eaten between meals) in Britain is the baked potato, or 'potato in its jacket', which is a potato cooked with the skin left on.

These are cut open and eaten with something on top like butter, cheese or beans. Supermarkets sell a lot of quick snacks and meals these days, like cup-a-soups to which you just add boiling water, or meals you can quickly heat up in the microwave

A quick snack   A supermarket sandwich

Fish and chips

from the Middle East. You may choose either to 'eat in' or 'take away'.

Sandwiches (either bought or home-made) make a quick lunch, and are easy to take to school or work. The word 'sandwich' comes from a man called John Montagu, the Fourth Earl of Sandwich who lived in the eighteenth century in the English town of Sandwich. He liked to play games at the table for a long time without stopping for a meal and so his cook put some beef between two pieces of bread – and made the first sandwich.

oven: very popular with people who do not like cooking!

You can buy many other kinds of hot fast food today, for example burgers and fried chicken from the USA, pizza from Italy, and kebabs

Baked potato with cheese and beans

7 Potatoes: a staple food

Although potatoes are one of the most important, or staple, foods in the British diet, they first came from South America. Farmers in Peru grew them from the thirteenth century on, and then the Spanish brought them back to Europe in the mid-sixteenth century. In the seventeenth century potatoes were introduced to the British Isles from mainland Europe and they became a very important crop in Ireland. Potatoes were so important in fact, that when the crops failed because of disease in 1845, 1846 and 1848, thousands of Irish people died because they did not have enough food to eat. Many other people moved to North America or Britain; and there are still many Irish people in Liverpool and other British cities today.

During the First and Second World Wars (1914–1918 and 1939–1945), it was difficult to bring fresh fruit and vegetables into Britain and so farmers grew a lot of potatoes. They still do.

Today the British grow six million tonnes of potatoes every year and most people eat over a hundred kilograms a year. Some potatoes have red skins, some white; sometimes they are eaten with the skin, sometimes without. There are many different kinds and many ways of cooking them, for example: boiling and mashing (with milk and butter), baking, roasting, and frying (using oil, for example chips).

You can also make potato soup, potato bread, potato salad, or use up extra cooked potatoes in a dish with the strange name of 'bubble and squeak'. To make this, take the cooked potatoes left over after a meal, mash them, mix them with some cooked cabbage and any other vegetables, and fry them with a little oil until golden brown. This is popular the day after a big roast dinner. The dish gets its name from the noises it sometimes makes when frying, and is often served with cold meat.

Potatoes

Potato masher

Mashed potatoes

Roast potatoes

We cannot talk about potatoes and not talk about one of Britain's favourite snacks: crisps. Over seven million packets of crisps are eaten in Britain every day! The first potato crisps were fried in the USA in 1852 but they were not made in Britain until the early 1900s. A food shop manager called Frank Smith started selling them in open paper bags from his bicycle in London in 1920. Then he found people liked salt on them so he put a small blue paper packet containing some salt in each bag of crisps.

Crisps became more popular during the Second World War because although it was difficult to get many kinds of food, potatoes could still be bought. Most supermarkets today sell many different types, like salted, salt and vinegar, cheese and onion, Worcester sauce, beef, and chicken.

8 A sweet tooth

Cakes, chocolate, ice-cream . . . the British love them all. A meal is not a full meal without some kind of dessert and sweet things are very popular as a snack too. Every shopping street has a baker's shop selling bread and cakes, and a newsagent's shop selling chocolate and ice-cream as well as newspapers.

Chocolate is the most popular sweet snack, and the British eat more than eight kilograms per person per year of it. Christopher Columbus, the Italian traveller (1451–1506), brought chocolate from Central America to Europe at the end of the fifteenth century but it was not really eaten in Britain until the mid-nineteenth century. The Cadbury family began to make drinking chocolate in Birmingham in 1831 and by 1878 they had 200 workers. They needed a bigger

Cakes

factory so they bought some land and built a new one. They also built a whole village for the workers, which they called Bournville. By 1881 they were selling chocolate as far away as Australia, and by 1899 they had more than 2,600 workers.

Chocolate is eaten almost anywhere, any time, but is very popular at Christmas and Easter. Dark chocolate, milk chocolate, white chocolate . . . there are many kinds to choose from, and British chocolate products are today sold all over the world.

Ice-cream is eaten as a snack, a dessert, or with another dessert (like a piece of hot apple pie). Traditionally it is made from milk, fat, sugar and things like fruit, nuts or mint, but today vegetable oils are often used instead of milk.

In the 1920s ice-cream was sold from three-wheeled bicycles called trikes, ridden by the ice-cream seller who shouted 'Stop me and buy one!' Then vans were used – they drove around the streets playing music so people would run out and buy some ice-cream.

Ice-cream is often eaten in cinemas and theatres, and children still go running for money when they hear the music played by the ice-cream van on a hot summer's day.

There are three main kinds of cooked desserts (also called puddings): baked puddings (cooked in the oven, for example, fruit pies), boiled or steamed puddings (cooked over boiling water, for example

A trifle

Christmas pudding), and milk or cream puddings (for example rice puddings). Cream is the fatty part of milk, it is darker in colour and tastes richer.

One of the most famous British desserts is the sherry trifle, served cold and usually made in a big glass bowl. On the bottom is some fruit, then some cake with sherry – a kind of strong wine – poured over. Then there is some red jelly, on top of that yellow custard, then cream, and finally nuts on top.

One of the most popular British summer desserts is also one of the simplest: fresh strawberries with thick cream on top.

An ice-cream van

9 Going for a drink

'See you in the Red Lion,' someone says to you. Yes, but which Red Lion? There are hundreds of pubs called the Red Lion, in fact it is the most popular pub name in Britain. Other names often used are The King's Head, The George (also named after a king), and The Plough.

Pubs (or public houses) are found in most towns and villages, and are often the centre of life in that area. People go there to have a drink, eat a meal, meet friends, listen to music and play games like darts

Pubs often have two bars, one

Buying a pint

A pub beer garden

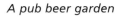

usually quieter than the other, and many have a garden where people can sit in the summer. Children can go in pub gardens with their parents, but can often only go inside a pub, with an adult, if they are over fourteen. Pubs can stay open from 11.00 am to 11.00 pm (or until 10.30 pm on Sundays) and are usually open 365 days a year.

Most pubs belong to a brewery (a company which makes beer) but sell many different kinds of beer, some

on tap (from a big container under the bar) and some in bottles. The most popular kind of British beer is bitter, which is dark and served at room temperature (not hot, not cold). More popular today though is lager, which is lighter in colour and served cold. Guinness, a very dark, creamy kind of beer called a stout, is made in Ireland and England and is very popular all over Britain.

In the West of England, cider, made from apples, is very popular. Like wine, it is described as sweet or dry, but it is drunk in beer glasses and can be stronger than beer.

While most food and drink in British supermarkets is now sold in litres and kilograms, beer and cider in pubs are still sold by the pint (a pint is 568 ml) or half pint.

Wine is also drunk in pubs and so are spirits (for example whisky, gin, rum and vodka). Spirits are usually drunk either 'on the rocks' (with ice) or with juice or a soft drink (for example whisky and soda, or gin and tonic).

People out with friends often order a round of drinks, so one person buys for everyone and then the next time someone else buys, and so on. One round could sound like this: 'A pint of best, half a dry cider, a dry white wine, and a G and T please.' In other words: a pint of best bitter beer, half a pint of dry cider, a glass of dry white wine, and a gin and tonic water. Someone wanting to drink the same thing again, says 'Same again, please.'

Playing darts

10   A nice cup of tea

It does not matter what the problem is, for the British the answer is often the same: 'Let's have a nice hot cup of tea.' Coffee has become very popular in Britain in recent years, but tea is still the national drink. Over 25 million cups of tea are sold every day, and many millions more are made at home.

In 1610 tea was brought from China to Europe. At first it was very expensive so not many people could buy it, but by 1750 it was widely drunk in Britain. By the late eighteenth century, Britain was at the centre of the world tea business and soon afterwards the tradition of taking afternoon tea, either at home or in a tea shop, began. Afternoon tea is a pot of tea, and a light snack (perhaps some small thin sandwiches and a piece of cake) served around four o'clock in the afternoon. A 'cream tea' is tea served with scones and cream, and you can find the recipe for scones at the end of this book.

Tea shops became popular with women because they could go there

A worker's tea-break

alone, to meet friends.

Since the mid-nineteenth century, tea has been brought to Britain from India, Africa and Sri Lanka as well as China. Today there are over 1,500 different kinds, for example Assam, Darjeeling, Oolong, Earl Grey and English Breakfast. Each one has a different smell and taste.

The traditional way of making tea is:
1   Boil some fresh cold water.
2   Put some hot water into the tea-pot to make it warm.

Milk and sugar?

has changed a lot in the last few years however. Most people now use tea-bags instead of tea-leaves because it is easier, and many use a mug instead of a cup and saucer. Tea is often made in the mug, without a pot (to save time) and many people no longer add milk and sugar.

Because tea-bags are so popular, the companies who sell them are always trying to make them better. At first tea-bags were square, then round ones were made, and now you can buy three-sided ones! Maybe the way people make tea has changed over the years but in this country of tea-drinkers, many people still use the old Chinese word for tea and like nothing better than to have a *cup of cha* or even just a good old *cuppa*.

3 Pour the water away.
4 Put one teaspoon of tea-leaves per person, and one extra tea-spoon, into the pot.
5 Pour boiling water onto the tea.
6 Leave for a few minutes.
7 Serve.

In the past, the usual way to serve tea was to put a little cold milk in a cup, pour the tea (using a tea-strainer – like a spoon with holes in it – to keep the tea-leaves out) and then add some sugar. Tea-making

Tea for two

11 How to make Shepherd's Pie

Pies are popular in Britain. There are many different kinds: some with meat, some with fish, some with fruit (for dessert). A shepherd is a person who looks after sheep, and a shepherd's pie is usually made from lamb. To make it for four people, you need:

900 g potatoes
45 ml milk (**a**)
50 g butter (**b**)
salt and pepper (**c**)
15 ml vegetable oil (**d**)
1 large onion (**e**)
150 ml stock (**f**)

450g cold cooked lamb, minced (cut in very small pieces)
30 ml dried herbs
g = grams,
ml = millilitres
This is what you do:

1 Turn the oven on to 190°C.
2 Cook the potatoes in boiling water with some salt in it for 15–20 minutes, until they are soft.
3 Mash the potato with the milk, butter, salt and pepper, using a fork or potato masher.

4 Heat the oil, add the onion and fry for about **5** minutes.
5 Add the meat, stock, salt and pepper and heat it all together.
6 Put the meat in a big bowl and cover with the potato.
7 Cook it for 25–30 minutes until brown on top.

If you use uncooked meat, cook it with the onion until brown. Enjoy your meal!

12 How to make Scones

Like pies, scones can be either sweet or savoury. They are often eaten with a cup of tea in the afternoon.

To make them, you need butter, milk, sugar and flour. The sugar you need here is a fine sugar called caster sugar, and the flour is self-raising, which means it makes the scones get bigger when they are cooking. Here is the list of things you need:

225 g self-raising flour
40 g butter
150 ml milk
20 ml caster sugar
salt

You also need a sieve (**a**), a mixing bowl (**b**), a rolling pin (**c**), a pastry cutter (**d**), a baking sheet (**e**) and a cooling rack (**f**).

1 Turn the oven to 220°C.
2 Push the flour through the sieve into a bowl and add the butter with your fingers.
3 Add the sugar and a little salt.
4 Using a knife, add the milk, little by little.
5 Make it into a ball with your hands. This is dough.
6 Roll the dough with the rolling pin until it is 1–2 cm thick.
7 Cut the dough using the cutter.
8 Put the scones onto the baking sheet.
9 Cook for 12–15 minutes until brown.
10 Put on the cooling rack until cool.
11 Eat with butter, jam and cream.

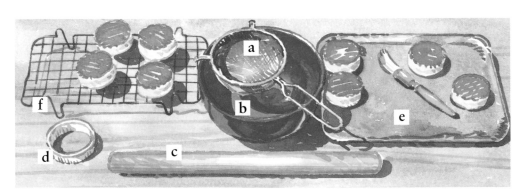

Exercises

A Checking your understanding

Pages 1–7 *Write the answers to these questions.*
1 What is Britain's national drink?
2 What don't vegetarians eat?
3 What brings in more money than fishing?

Pages 8–13 *Are these sentences true (T) or false (F)?*
1 'B & B' means 'bed and bath'.
2 There are over 8,000 Indian restaurants in Britain.
3 Caerphilly cheese is from Wales.

Pages 16–21 *Can you remember the answers to these questions?*
1 What is a potato in its jacket?
2 What is 'bubble and squeak' made from?
3 When is chocolate the most popular in Britain?

Pages 22–27 *Choose the right answer.*
1 What is the most popular pub name: 'The Red Lion' or 'The King's Head'?
2 What is the traditional way to serve tea in Britain: with milk or lemon?
3 What kind of meat is used to make shepherd's pie: lamb or pork?
4 What do people serve scones with: jam or marmalade?

B Working with language

1 *Use these words to join the two sentences together.*
   and   but   because   so   then
   1 Today we have more foods to choose from. We have less time for shopping and cooking.
   2 In the hills it rains more. The grass grows well and there are more sheep.

3 Beef is eaten with horseradish sauce. Lamb is eaten with mint sauce.
4 Tea was very expensive at first. It was brought from China.
5 Heat the oil. Fry the onion.

2 *Put together these beginnings and endings of sentences and check your answers on pages 26–7.*

1 Cook the potatoes . . .
2 If you use uncooked meat . . .
3 Using a knife . . .
4 Cut the dough . . .

5 cook it with the onion.
6 until they are soft.
7 using the cutter.
8 add the milk

3 *Put these sentences about making tea in the right order and check your answers on pages 24–5.*

1 Pour the water away.
2 Pour boiling water onto the tea.
3 Boil some fresh cold water.
4 Put some hot water into the tea-pot.
5 Put one teaspoon of tea-leaves per person into the pot.

C Activities

1 Think of a wonderful or terrible meal you have had and describe it. Where were you and who were you with? Why was it so good or so bad?
2 It is your birthday and a friend wants to take you out to eat. What kind of food would you like? Which restaurant would you choose and why?

D Project Work

Congratulations! You have just opened a restaurant which serves food traditional in your country. Choose a name for your restaurant, then:
1 Write the menu.
2 Choose one dish and write the recipe.

Glossary

agree to think the same way as someone

boil cook in very hot water

cheese type of food made from milk, can be hard or soft

cider adult drink made from apples

dish a kind of food, for example 'fish and chips'

Earl a title, like Mr, or Dr

electricity used to make things like a fridge or washing machine work

fat soft oily part of some plants and animals

fresh just made (like *fresh tea*) or recently picked (like *fresh fruit*)

fry cook something in oil

gas (*n*) used by some people for cooking and heating their homes

government the group of people who control a country

herb fresh or dry plant used to give food extra taste

marmalade made from oranges; you put it on toast

mash (*n/v*) cook vegetables, like potatoes, until soft then press together

national something which belongs to the whole country

oven a place in the kitchen, using gas or electric, that you cook food in

pollution something which makes the air, land or water unhealthy

recipe an explanation of how to cook something

serve to give people food or drink

spice part of a plant with a sharp or sweet taste

stock (*n*) water in which meat, fish or vegetables are cooked for a long time

tradition an old way of doing something

vinegar a strong tasting liquid used to flavour food

war big fight between two or more countries

wine adult drink made from grapes